Run, Cat,

On Sam's bed is a hat...

A big red hat.

And in that hat is a cat…

A big fat cat.

And on Sam's bed is a tin…

A big, big tin.

Sam hit the tin for fun...

Run, cat, run!

Hey, Man, You Bet I Can!

Can a dog hop on a wall?

Can the sun play with a ball?

Can a van have a hat on top?

Can a cat sit on a mop?

Can a hen get sad?

Can a bug get mad?

Can a fat rat tap?

Can a red fox rap?